WHO WAS

ERNEST JUST?

The Story of a Biologist

Biography Book for Kids Grade 5 | Children's Biographies

DISSECTED LIVES
auto biographies

First Edition, 2020

Published in the United States by Speedy Publishing LLC, 40 E Main Street, Newark, Delaware 19711 USA.

Dissected Lives Books are available at special discounts when purchased in bulk for industrial and sales-promotional use. For details contact our Special Sales Team at Speedy Publishing LLC, 40 E Main Street, Newark, Delaware 19711 USA. Telephone (888) 248-4521 Fax: (210) 519-4043.

10 9 8 7 6 * 5 4 3 2 1

Print Edition: 9781541953857
Digital Edition: 9781541956858

See the world in pictures. Build your knowledge in style.
www.speedypublishing.com

CONTENTS

Ernest Everett Just

Ernest Everett Just may not be a household name, but his contributions to the field of cellular biology established some important foundations for the field. As an African American scientist in the early 1900s, Just had to overcome prejudices because of his race and constantly had to prove his academic intelligence amid a sea of white scientists. Just's work, while groundbreaking, was often scrutinized by the American scientific community[1]. In this book, we will look at the life and work of Ernest Just, as well as the obstacles he overcame to advance his scientific work. Let's get started.

---

[1] Scientific Community – A network of scientists working collaboratively.

ERNEST JUST'S CHILDHOOD

Ernest Everett Just was born in Charleston, South Carolina, on August 14, 1883. His father, Charles Frazier Just, died when he was only four years old, leaving his mother, Mary Matthews Just, to raise him on her own. Mary Just, a schoolteacher, struggled to support her little family.

Historical downtown area of Charleston, South Carolina, USA

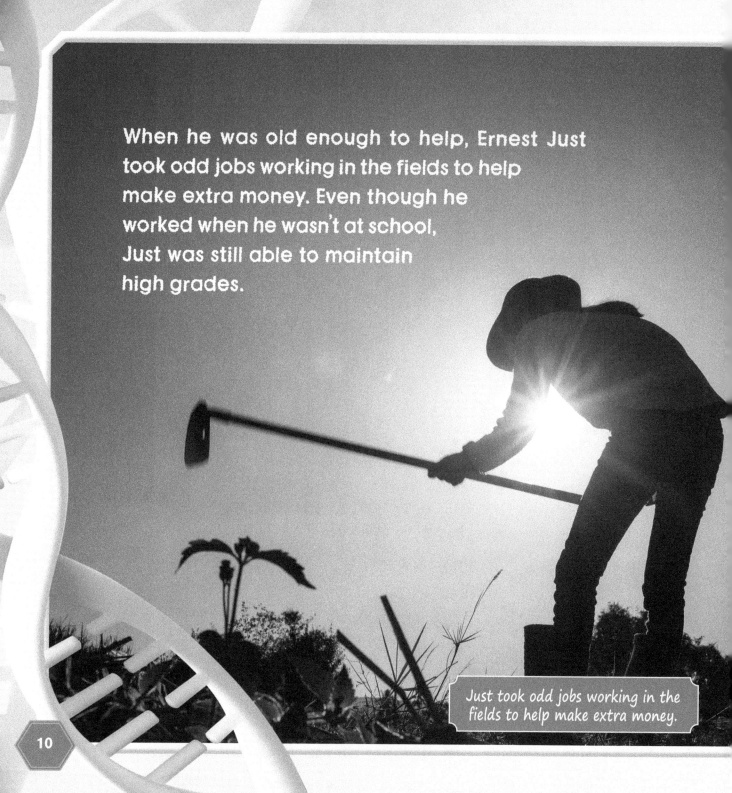

When he was old enough to help, Ernest Just took odd jobs working in the fields to help make extra money. Even though he worked when he wasn't at school, Just was still able to maintain high grades.

Just took odd jobs working in the fields to help make extra money.

When he was 17, Just and his mother had a serious discussion about his future academic career. They decided that Just would get a stronger education if he were to attend a school in the North after he graduated from high school in Charleston.

THE EDUCATION OF ERNEST JUST

Ernest Just and his mother did their research and decided that the private Kimball Union Academy in New Hampshire would be the best option for him to continue his education. The problem was, he had no money for tuition.

Kimball Union Academy in Meriden, New Hampshire

At just 17 years old, Ernest Just left home to go to New York City in hopes of finding a job that paid more money than farm work. He only needed one month in New York to earn enough money to pay his tuition at Kimball Academy.

Manhattan and Brooklyn Bridge in New York City

Just was able to finish four years' worth of schoolwork in three years.

Once enrolled there, Just worked hard on his coursework. In fact, he was able to finish four years' worth of work in only three years. In addition to doubling up on his studies, Just was the president of Kimball Academy's debate team and the editor of the school's newspaper.

JUST AT DARTMOUTH COLLEGE

When he graduated from Kimball Academy, Ernest Just enrolled in Dartmouth College. He chose Dartmouth intentionally. Of all the Ivy League schools in the country, Dartmouth was the most open to accepting African American students.

Dartmouth College in Hanover, New Hampshire, USA

Just faced his share of discrimination and racial stereotyping as a student at Dartmouth.

In fact, Dartmouth welcomed its first group of African American students in 1775, 128 years before Just's time there. Still, he faced his share of discrimination and racial stereotyping as a student at Dartmouth.

However, it was at Dartmouth that Just was introduced to biology. He graduated at the top

Dartmouth University Class of 1907

of his class...the only magna cum laude[2] student
in the Dartmouth class of 1907.

2   Magna Cum Laude – Latin for "with great honor", it is presented to students
    graduating with very high grade point averages.

THE MARINE BIOLOGICAL LABORATORY

Beginning in 1909, Just trained in biology every summer at the Marine Biological Laboratory, or MBL, in Massachusetts, studying under the facility's director, Frank R. Lillie, who was also the chair of the Zoology Department at the University of Chicago.

Frank R. Lillie

Marine Biological Laboratory,
Woods Hole, Massachusetts

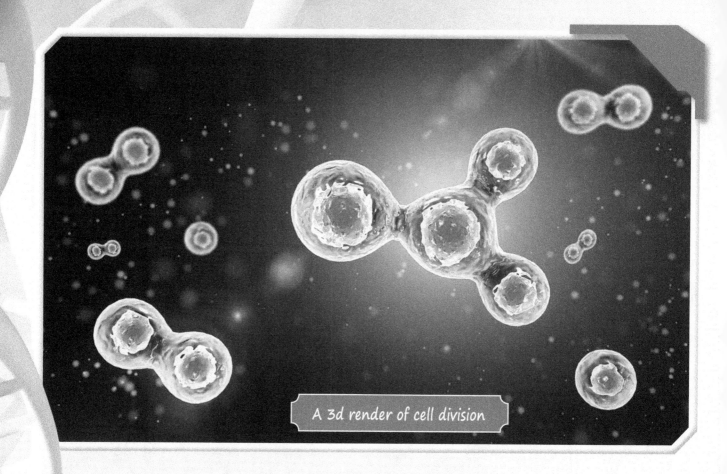

A 3d render of cell division

Lillie challenged Just to research cell division[3], particularly in marine organisms. This sparked Just's passion for cellular biology and his theories on cell cleavage and fertilization.

3   Cell Division – How cells reproduce and grow

In 1912, Just wrote and published his first scientific paper on the subject, "The Relation of the First Cleavage Plane to the Entrance Point of the Sperm." Later scientists viewed this work as the generally accepted authority on the subject.

Just wrote and published his first scientific paper in 1912.

THE RELATION OF THE FIRST CLEAVAGE PLANE TO THE ENTRANCE POINT OF THE SPERM.*

ERNEST E. JUST.

During the summer of 1911 at the Marine Biological Laboratory under the direction of Professor Frank R. Lillie, I was engaged in the study of the eggs of *Nereis* of certain cytological problems the results of which will appear later. The question of the relation of the entrance-point of the sperm and the first cleavage plane occurred to me. A very pretty method made possible in a satisfactory fashion the determination of this relation the results of which this paper embodies. I here take this opportunity to express my thanks and sense of gratitude to Professor Lillie for his inspiring interest in the work of which this is a part.

MATERIAL AND METHODS.

The eggs of *Nereis* when shed a~~~~
pressure while in the ~~~~
the sea~~~~

RACIAL TENSION AT MBL

Although Ernest Just's work was shining a positive light on the research being done at the MBL, Just was enduring racial prejudice.

Just endured racial prejudice at the MBL.

For example, when a new clubhouse was built on the grounds of the MBL to be a meeting place for the MBL Club, Just was asked not to attend the building's dedication or any other social gathering at the clubhouse.

Just's experience at the MBL left him frustrated, angry, and bitter.

His boss and mentor, Lillie, wanted to offer Just a permanent position at the lab, but he bowed to pressure from others who did not want to see an African American hired in a full-time position. In all, his experience at the MBL left Just frustrated, angry, and bitter.

1.1983457

0.0081243

1.1892656

1.0128639

1

0.9812652

1.3478651

ERNEST JUST, SCIENTIST

Even with his impressive academic record, Ernest Just could not get a position at a traditional university. He was hired to teach at an all-black college, Howard University, where he could continue his research into cellular biology and cell division.

Howard University Founders Library building in Washington, DC

University of Chicago in Chicago, Illinois, USA

After his time at Massachusetts' Woods Hole Marina Biological Laboratory, Just planned to obtain his doctorate degree. He enrolled in the University of Chicago to study embryology[4] and graduated magna cum laude with his Doctor of Philosophy degree.

4   Embryology – The science dealing with the foundation, development, and structure of embryos.

JUST'S PIONEERING WORK

During his doctorate work, Ernest Just made a number of key contributions to the field of cellular biology and cell development. He researched how cells divide, with and without fertilization. He also experimented on the effects of radiation, ultraviolet rays, and various carcinogens[5] on cells.

Just experimented on the effects of radiation, ultraviolet rays, and various carcinogens on cells.

5 Carcinogen – A cancer causing agent

In the emerging field of cellular biology, Just helped to advance the basic understanding of cell physiology. He wrote and published his findings, particularly "General Cytology", which was published in 1924.

GENERAL CYTOLOGY

A TEXTBOOK OF CELLULAR STRUCTURE AND FUNCTION FOR STUDENTS OF BIOLOGY AND MEDICINE

By

ROBERT CHAMBERS
EDWIN G. CONKLIN
EDMUND V. COWDRY
MERKEL H. JACOBS
ERNEST E. JUST
MARGARET R. LEWIS

WARREN H. LEWIS
FRANK R. LILLIE
RALPH S. LILLIE
CLARENCE E. McCLUNG
ALBERT P. MATHEWS
THOMAS H. MORGAN
EDMUND B. WILSON

Edited by
EDMUND V. COWDRY

"General Cytology" published in 1924

JUST HAD
TO BE
RESPECTFUL

The theories Ernest Just developed and research that he did were shared with the scientific community, a standard practice then as it is now. Because of his race, however, the work that Just produced was subject to extra scrutiny[6]. Many people during Just's lifetime truly believed that African Americans were not as smart or capable as their white counterparts, therefore some of Just's colleagues hoped to find errors in Just's methods and calculations so they could reinforce their own prejudices.

6   Scrutiny – Closely watch and analyze, looking for errors.

The theories Just developed and research that he did were shared with the scientific community.

When his research was challenged by other scientists, Just knew he had to respond in a humble and respectful way, or risk damaging his reputation. When Just himself wanted to debate the validity of ideas and theories put forth by white biologists, he had to do so in a polite, unpretentious way so that he did not appear "uppity".

Just had to respond in a humble and respectful way when his research was challenged by other scientists.

ERNEST JUST'S PERSONAL LIFE

Just's first wife, Ethel, and their three children from left to right: Highwarden, Maribel and Margaret.

O n June 26, 1912, Ernest Just got married to a young high school teacher named Ethel Highwarden. The couple had two daughters, Margaret and Maribel, and a son named Highwarden. Just remained married to Ethel until 1939 when he filed for divorce, and soon after, married his second wife, Hedwig Schnetzler, a young student studying philosophy in Berlin where Just was then living. The late 1930s and early 1940s was a tough time for a black American to be living in Germany.

In 1940, Just was sent to a Nazi camp for a brief time but was released after his new wife's father intervened on his behalf. Just and his bride fled to France and later had a daughter, Elisabeth.

Male prisoners in a Nazi camp.

1.1983457

0.0981243

1.1892656

1

0.9812652

1.0128639

1.3478651

AN AWARD-WINNING SCIENTIST

The National Association for the Advancement of Colored People, or NAACP, established its annual Spingarn Medal in 1914 to recognize the outstanding achievements by an African American person. The award committee selected Ernest Just to be the very first recipient of Spingarn Award in 1915 to honor the work he was doing in the field of cellular biology. In addition, Just was appointed to serve as editor of three different prestigious academic journals, which was a nod to his professional accomplishments.

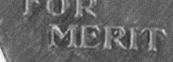

The Spingarn Medal

Just was appointed to serve as editor of three different prestigious academic journals.

1.1983457

0.09⎵⎵43

1.1892656

1

0.98⎵2652

1.0128639

1.3478651

JUST TRAVELS TO EUROPE

Ernest Just was named the Julius Rosenwald Fellow in Biology by the National Research Council, a position he held from 1920 to 1931. This fellowship[7] allowed him to travel to Europe and work with many of the top European biologists. He found that the European scientists treated him like an equal, unlike many of his American colleagues.

National Academies of Sciences, Engineering, and Medicine and the National Research Council, Washington D.C., USA

---

7   Fellowship – An academic scholarship or award to provide support for a student doing advanced studies.

The racial discrimination of the day that was an obstacle to Just's career advancement in the United States was not as much of a factor in Europe. He found a community of like-minded scientists and the freedom to devote his time to his research. Some of his most significant work, including his 1924 research paper "General Cytology", was done during this time.

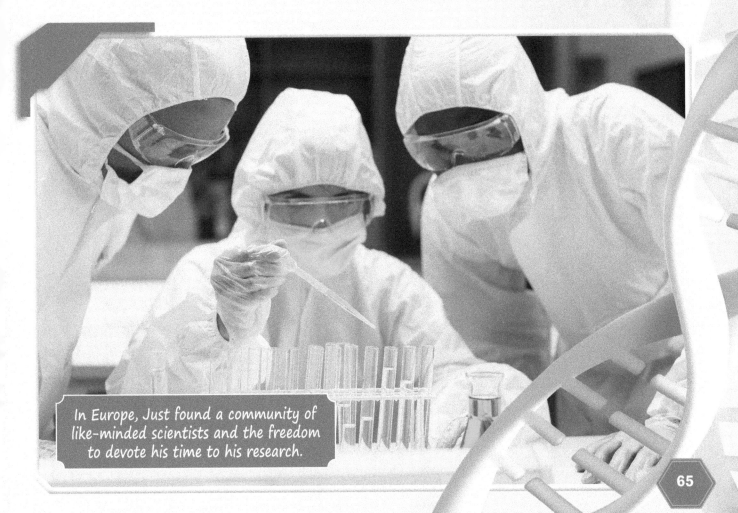

In Europe, Just found a community of like-minded scientists and the freedom to devote his time to his research.

SELF-
IMPOSED
EXILE

Kaiser Wilhelm Institute for Physics in Berlin, Germany

Even after his fellowship ended, Ernest Just remained in Europe in what he called a self-imposed exile. He worked at various scientific laboratories, such as the Kaiser Wilhelm Institute in Berlin, Germany, the Stazione Zoologica in Naples, Italy, and the Station Biologique in Roscoff, France.

Stazione Zoologica in Naples, Italy

Station Biologique in Roscoff, France

In addition to his membership in several scientific societies in the United States — including the American Society of Zoologists, the American Ecological Society, the American Society of Naturalists, and the American Association for the Advancement of Science — Just joined the Societe Nationale des Sciences Naturelles et Mathematiques de Cherbourg.

American Association for the Advancement of Science in Washington, DC.

Headquarters of the Societe Nationale des Sciences Naturelles et Mathematiques de Cherbourg in France

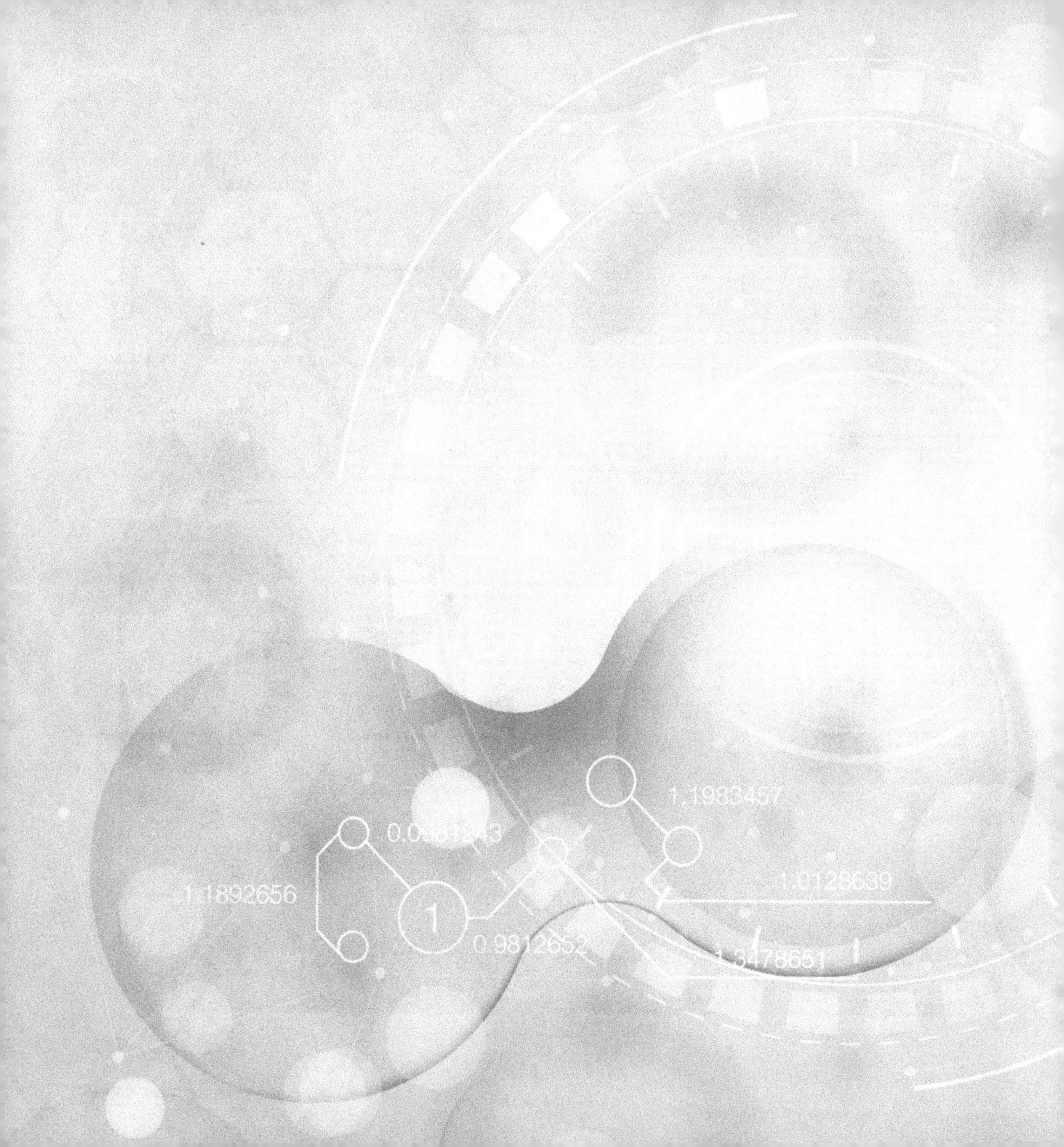
1.1983457
1.1892656
1
0.9812652
1.0128639
1.3478651

FLEEING EUROPE

S.S. Excambion

After Ernest Just was freed from the Nazi camp and journeyed to France with his new wife, the couple tried to travel to the United States, but they ran into several obstacle. They left France for Spain, and then Portugal, before securing passage on the S.S. Excambion.

Just was in poor health and Hedwig was pregnant, making the journey across the Atlantic a miserable one. Back on American soil, Just returned to teaching at Howard University, the place that gave him his first job after college.

Just returned to teaching at Howard University.

By July of 1941, Just's stomach ailment had become so debilitating that he was admitted to the hospital. He was diagnosed with pancreatic cancer and died a few months later, on October 27, 1941.

Ernest Everett Just's grave in Lincoln Memorial Cemetery, Suitland, Prince George's County, Maryland, USA

SUMMARY

As an African American scientist living in the early 1900s, Ernest Just had to be more than intelligent. He also had to be careful not to upstage white scientists, many of whom harbored resentment toward the brilliant Just. He took his impressive educational and research background across the Atlantic to Europe when he found a welcoming scientific community. His research in the area of cell biology and fertilization laid the groundwork for biological studies that are still being done today.

There are many African American scientists whose work was vital to their fields, but whose names were overshadowed because of their race. Now that you know the accomplishments of Ernest Just and how he had to overcome prejudice to advance in his field, you are ready to learn about other, equally brilliant African American scientists.

Visit

www.speedypublishing.com

To view and download free content on your favorite subject and browse our catalog of new and exciting books for readers of all ages.

CPSIA information can be obtained
at www.ICGtesting.com
Printed in the USA
BVHW062049280121
599006BV00005B/420